We Like Weddings

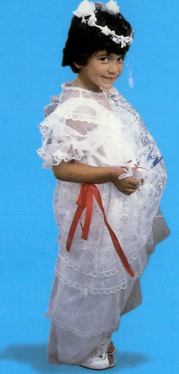

Written by Antony Lishak

We like weddings.

We wear special clothes
at weddings.

5

We carry flowers at weddings.

We hold cushions at weddings.

We carry candles at weddings.

We blow shells at weddings.

13

We like weddings.

15

Glossary

candle

clothes

cushion

flowers

shell